Oh, Soft Winged Psyche

Poetry Crafted in the Style of a Murder Mystery

Regan Frioux

BookLeaf Publishing
India | USA | UK

Made with ❤ on the BookLeaf Publishing Platform
www.bookleafpub.in
www.bookleafpub.com

Dedication

To my family- my mom and stepdad especially- for always believing in me.

Preface

I knew I was going to do this challenge again, and originally planned to submit a random assortment of poems. What I didn't know, however, was that I was about to scrap all of those poems and write 21 poems to a plot of a murder mystery during the the busiest semester in college of my life. So, that was fun.

No, but really, it was. As I was writing the characters and watching them come together, I had this sense of "wow" and I hope everyone who reads this also "wows" the same way.

I'll stop yapping and let you read on- enjoy!

Acknowledgements

Special thank you to my cat, who lets me squeeze his little cheeks in times of stress. He can't read but he knows I love him, trust me.

Also thank you to my mom and stepdad who, beyond everything, step out of their way to make sure I am always feeling supported and loved.

Big Thank You to my friends!! Who either had to listen to thousands of ideas being bounced off them, were forced to edit these poems, or were just there to be my friend.

Love you all!!

1. The Party

At the edge of the world, it seems like,
she stands on an open canvas
of oranges and blues and purples.
Virtue looks out at the setting sun,
fingertip flirting with the lip of her drink–
barely sipped.
She leans on the railing, refraining from
a downward gaze.
(If anyone were to fall, it would surely be a
hundred foot drop).

A halo of people hums around her,
the pretty buzzing of a bee.
A sweet, honeyed symphony.
Someone idles next to her.
But, oh, she doesn't pay them much mind.
Virtue prefers the hum of the bees–
Just an arms reach away–
their carriage to pollinate,
a strictly social affair.

And minutes later, well, nobody knows what happened.
They just heard the screaming.

All tangled and twisted,
what Virtue would call the eye of the hive,
Vice skirts from comrade to confidant.
A hand on a shoulder,
trickling down an arm to the small of a back.
Slithering,
a snake to a charmer- or the charmer himself.
Quickfingers make for a
quicker getaway
fingers coiling around a jewel.

How very intimate it is,
draped in silk and gold.
A breath as faint as the breeze, sliding over
just the right amount of exposed skin.
On a collarbone- behind an ear. (Don't tell).
The drinks are sweet enough,
and Vice's empty glasses litter the floor.

Another one hits the concrete when the crowd scatters
towards the edge.

2. The Interrogation #1: Vice

9:04

So did you know the victim? .

The clock pounds and pounds,
the running of feet.
the beating of a hammer
on concrete– on a head.
Vice is not so elegant as he was an hour ago,
working out a knot in his left temple,
his hand then falling limply,
haphazardly, in disarray.

I'm not even sure why I'm here, my dear.

His voice drawls on an extra syllable,
tongue catching on his teeth when
he isn't expecting it.
Fingers scratch condemnation into
the worn wooden table,
itching to reach further.

Nice watch–

Is it real?

You don't remember?

'Traitor, Justice,'
the table wants to speak.
A judge with his gavel,
pounding.
As the clock begins its rounds again.
a smile carves rounded cheeks–
completely on accident–
innocently, a bystander to calamity.

You have to understand, I was rather drunk...

Apathy is dead. They were pushed from the roof.

A number of things fall in this moment:

- The room, silent
- The smile on Vice's face (if only for a moment before growing again)
- The sun
- The image of Apathy in Vice's head

3. Interrogation #1: Virtue

10:47

Studying the bricks as if
the moon will creep through the cracks,
some dreamy, elegant light.
Instead, a harshness radiates from the
fluorescents.
A flickering, a buzzing–
though lacking the lingering promise
of honey.

So, you were next to the victim when
it happened?

But how could anyone claim
the bees' honey as their own?
(To humans, to bears).
A communion of sweets,
a give and take. When death
had to befall a whole colony to achieve it.
(If humans grew claws, of course).

Virtue searches for the moon
in the eyes before her.

The same swinging between her own–
inquiring, tense.
Swinging between three and nine
back to three, then to six, looking for an answer.

Apathy? Yes, I was next to them when they... fell.

4. The Olive Tree

A little more than a few years into youth, Virtue climbs the branch of a tree. Picking olives from foliage, popping them into her mouth, pinching the stems between her nails. And the olive tree creaks as if in pain. And the olive explodes in her mouth.

Some would say the olive tree collects wisdom—it groans, creaks, and aches with the knowledge it gathers. Virtue is not the first to eat an olive; Virtue would not be the first to ignore the tree.

A few days later, Virtue witnesses a caterpillar inch across a rickety branch. It teeters on an unsteady path– just a baby– its first light, its first steps. It reaches an olive and digs into its flesh. The olive spits out juice, lets it trickle down its sides, and the olive tree creaks and lets the olive tumble to the floor.

Sitting on a branch, Virtue envisions the caterpillar on the ground and the olive tree and herself atop it, and she wonders.

5. The Robin

A hundred and forty-five in his pockets and one more rolling between Vice's fingers. Gold, glinting in the high noon. What started off as a bet quickly became an addiction. A bump of the shoulder, a quick slip into a purse. There's no cure for kleptomania.

Vice lived for it, that split-second realization–
When they turned,oved the way they turned, reaching for their wallet and finding nothing but air. He loved it even more when they chased, when they crashed—stumbling and rolling—old joints and all.

Mothers and children, store owners and beggars—one in particular, who holds out his hands, a shiny gleam in his pupils.

A robin flaps its wings and Vice watches a caterpillar crash– stumble and roll– to the concrete just before him. Poor bird, to go hungry, and poor beggar, for the same reason. A hundred and fifty in his pockets now.

The robin took off again, its wings slicing through the air, his feet gliding on the brick-lined streets. The weight of the world seemed lighter when stolen– a hundred and fifty-one now.

6. Interrogation #2: Vice

9:15

Pushed? Really pushed?

It's an ugly sight–laughter–
one with spit flying and
a wheezing inhale. A swirling
epiphany. A monstrous cacophony.
A cough and a groan, Vice holds a hand to
his temple. The clock starts ticking again.

Yes– I need you to tell me
what you know.

Haven't we been over this?
Like I told you,
I was quite drunk.

And around the hand goes,
languidly roaming,
flickering from side to side.
Something about them was–
oh, would it be ironic to say 'apathetic?'
Lethargic fits best here.

There was a party, and we drank and danced.
I may have talked to Apathy,
But I'm a friend to all!

And there's a breath against his ear,
a soft one, a whimper of a
plead. Some faraway cry,
as if it were falling to its doom already.

You may have?

What is whispered is a secret,
Isn't it?

And boy, isn't it a nag
to have to deal with.
This oncoming headache.
An annoyance at its best–
the pleading. Bothersome
to pass by the railing
and picture the worst.

7. Interrogation #2: Virtue

11:02

How were they acting?

I can't say I was paying much
attention to them.

And who does? The little
one floating around soundless.
A heavy fog sat on the air,
and even so now–staler–
so maybe the sun looked like a dream.

Virtue wasn't looking at the sun,
though, remember?
Not in this instant.
The bees, the crowd.
Such a soundless approach,
and Virtue admired anything but.
(An accident, innocently).

So, you ignored them.

Ignore is a heavy word.

Surely, not heavier than
sacrifice. Redemption, even.
Many things come with weight.
Guilt– the eyes that
were unable to witness.
Versus the eyes who sat
atop the tree watching.

8. Interrogation: Ignorance

7:47

He ambles on a wire
straight through the crowd.
Swaying, a barking animal of laughter.
Two arms slung around
a secret arrangement.
Whispers behind an ear–
a moth flitting around catlike slits.

There was a party? I wasn't invited!

Multiple witnesses say otherwise.

If only arts and crafts were
so simple.
watching the thread unravel-
beads tumble, glass breaks
and glimmers and skids to the edge
of the building.
And Ignorance would see.

I didn't do anything wrong.

Obviously.

Nobody is saying you did.

He ambles on a wire
back through the crowd.
You can't undo many things.
Death is an example,
nothing more than an example.

A drink tingles on his lips,
the dog will howl in excitement
and others (in fear)
will inevitably follow.
But who was the first
to witness the moon?

9. The Storm.

The wind would blow, and the rain would pelt alongside it as a message. Maybe there would be lightning, strangely attracted to trees, their delicate foliage, and far too flammable bark—how long does it take for a tree to die?

But what you wouldn't notice at first was the ones who blend in. The ones who blend in– camouflage, they call it– with spotted gray and brown backs blend into the tree. They hide from predators, birds– robins– but not so much an unprecedented, unseen, unthought-of strike of lightning.

Virtue watches the cremation. A soul tied to a wooden post stuck in the ground. Virtue watches the fire grow, even in the rain, a torturous death (the price of having knowledge).

In the morning, after a full night of wind and rain, Virtue would mourn at the husk of an olive tree. Buried in the mud and the ash surrounding her knees are the ones you couldn't see. Their wings burned off, and their bodies with spotted gray and brown backs turned black. Without wings, they fell, and without wings, they crawled.

Should Virtue have ever looked down, she would have wondered, who took longer to die? Or rather, could she have helped?

10. Interrogation: Hypocrisy

8:20

I'd never associate with anyone
Capable of murder!

The first steps into the
afternoon breeze
make for a runway entrance.
Hypocrisy stalks in circles,
away from the quiet loners
near the edge of the hive.
From jubilant laughter at the
arm of a beautiful man to
a sneer at his wife's abhorrent lipstick.

The second steps into the
afternoon breeze– the third, the fourth–
are just as freeing as they should be.
Dressed in silk that moves as she does,
sitting still would-
well, Hypocrisy doesn't sit still.

Do you have any information?

I'm here to help in any way I can.
Apathy and I were close friends.

A picture of perfect poise,
candid, unmoving,
the way she liked to be seen.
Through the lens of a camera.
With her legs crossed, she sits unmoving.
She glances at the blinking red light.

Did Apathy talk to anyone?

Well,
Apathy wasn't the easiest person to get
along with.

The red blinking light,
illuminates against the red smeared
on her neck, her collar,
against the side of her lip.
What a beautiful shade it was.

11. The Wildfire.

The thing about fire, Vice learned, is that it spreads quickly. Violent as it is, it can be just as delicate. The thing about fire is that it can exist as a spark. To view a spark, though, is an interpretation of the mind–- a spark behind the eye is brilliant, a spark in the night sky is just as brilliant in death.

Languidly, the flame sways to a song without a beat. To know Vice is to understand that a song without a beat is lifeless– pounding feet, a hammer on concrete, on a head. And so the wax drips, burning through a pair of wings (innocent bystander). And so Vice knocks the candle over to set the house ablaze.

And so down goes the walls and the roof and the orchard outside. Down goes their riches, their gold into his pockets for which they will no longer flaunt (if they could). Flares fly up as Vice wanders off, and the spark reminds him.

While they were circumstantial, the moth would have died anyway.

12. Interrogation #3: Virtue

11:14

They are born to rule,
at least, they think they are.
Caressed with honey,
a mother's touch,
an overzealous hand.
In rare circumstances
one daughter is not enough
for a mother.
And they must fight to the death
to rule.

I was looking at the crowd,
you must understand
how fascinating bees are.

Bees?

And so the crowd erupts.
The hive sputters.
A runway darling,
a comedian's laughter,
a snake charmer (or the snake).

The hive buzzes, clashes.

Well, compared to a Moth.

A cloud, fog,
like smoke from a fire,
Apathy flickers around the edges.
And who would notice
the smoke when the flame
is so close to your skin.

The hive or a moth.
The glint of gold to
the interviewers' empty wrist.
A queen to another queen.

When I turned around Apathy was gone.

13. Interrogation #3: Vice

9:32

Vice would run in circles,
octagons, dodecahedrons,
before he admitted to the spur
of death.
To lose, a shame.
Though, Vice could not deny
the yearn to conspire.

The queen is the goal
and pawns start the game.
to play is to be insatiable,
winning is to have eaten your fill.
A platter of guts splayed before you,
artfully displayed, a stoup in waiting.

As if I would deny someone
their freedoms.

Murder is freedom?

A path diagonally,
forwards and backwards.

Straight through the pawns,
a knife clean through a limb.
Not many would mind the blood,
the decadence of the pour, the drip.
Red into a decanter.
Vice might mind a stain on his
freshly pressed collar.
But a push, a fall, prevents all of that.

Hah! For many!
Not me, in this instance,
of course.

14. Interrogation: Compassion

12:35 AM

She had no time to echo condolences,
so she mutters them now.
Fingers hold tight onto their sisters,
clasped in a cold embrace.
Compassion has held every
heavy heart. A stranger's beat
soothed by a companion's lullaby.
To grieve is so familiar, the next
one knocking at the door after love.

And you two were close?

I sought to feel, whereas
Apathy sought otherwise.
Though, I harbored no ill will.

The sticky points of glue,
of sap and honey that bind,
of warm bodies mingling too tight together.
The shouting, like a battlehorn.
A bird call over a mountain,

a peacock's feathers.

Compassion would glide along
a narrow path. Shallow waters,
slowly raising as the moon permits it.
Compassion would attempt to
show them the moon.
And the night comes anyway, the shadows rise–
Compassion would attempt to know
the moth.
But the moth would pass right by the shadows.

It's difficult when someone
doesn't seem to care about anything.

Difficult...?

That doesn't make them undeserving of care.

And the moth would wander to the edge.
And Compassion would wring her hands,
unaware.
The moon could crawl through the cracks
of the wall,
but the moon doesn't know a thing.
Wish for light or knowledge,
one of them will best suit.

Compassion wrings her hands, unaware.

Maybe we all ignored Apathy too much.

15. The Moth and the Butterfly.

And she would move to her like a woman to God, kneel before her like a child before stained glass. For all that keeps a Chapel lit, lanterns or candles, the sunlight through rouge or violet finds her someplace divine.

They would love each other further past temptation, hold each other someplace higher than a steeple, hold each other too close to the sun so that she could witness purity. Wings would collide at the fall, and glass would shatter at the impact.

They would sleep bundled in a dream, but the glass has shattered and that's all she understood. Apathy would wander to some greater wildfire, and Compassion would be left wondering how to piece together her colorful wings.

16. Capable.

For some, it is easier than others. A knife in his hands like a plea, a wish. A decision so simple it's rather a will, twisting through his heart like poison ivy. A weed that can still petal, so you let it live until it invades your garden until you pick one and your hand starts to bleed.

A mechanical fly without any real purpose. And he would sting to threaten, kill for the game. And the garden would bleed, and the petals wilt and fall– something in the remaining soil. With him, the juice drips from a cherry, coating his hands sweet and red.

For others, there is silence before the hymn, an omen of justice or sacrifice. And the gavel falls on a sob, a windy last exhale, she chokes out an atonement. Like water smoothing stone, over time, nothing will be left—yet the water remembers.

And she floats along, tired. The hand that pulled away took her entirety with it. The wind whispers once more, and it brings only the scent of nectar– she tastes only the bitterness of what remains. Soaking in the river, she misses the warmth of honey and her mother, for that was the price.

17. Interrogation #4: Virtue

11:24

You must have seen something.
Know something.

The air is too dry,
and she pulls at her collar.
The vents blow brisk air,
nipping at her fingers–
A tactic made to concern,
to disorient. A bee without
A line of sight.
They don't survive in the winter.

Sure, I acquaint myself with some
suspicious characters.

Vice would approach her later
and show off his new watch.
He wouldn't suppress a bubbling laugh
or the entertained gaze at the rooftop.

An easy road to follow, as roads go.
Yet, Virtue knows his stop all too well,

she was watching him
(probably too closely)
as he fell into a new woman's shoulder.
She watched him hold her between his fingers,
then set her aflame as if he'd be addicted
soon enough.
Virtue watches his old flames die out around him, herself
included,
the hive buzzing with contempt–
and then she turned.

But I assure you, if I saw anything
I would bring them forth.

And you?

And the sun was just passing
the skyline.
Wrapped up in clouds–
and it really looked like a dream,
as if you could reach out and touch it.

And when I turned, I saw the sun.
And then I look down, and
I saw Apathy.

Isn't the first to see them

the most guilty?

18. Interrogation #4: Vice

You must have seen something.
Know something.

How much weight does gold hold
when it ticks?
What about when it ticks a second faster
than the clock on the wall?
Vice can't watch it, really,
the second hand on his wrist,
(Slitted eyes are most often aimed
at the prey).
But he can hear it ticking, ticking.

Do I get a prize if I have?

Justice?

Then no, I haven't seen a thing.

He will show it to Virtue,
ask if she will buy it for double.
Then his eyes will wander,
squinted in a smile, a hidden laugh,
to a place where a ghost will remain.

A wanderer's street, a graveyard.
And she would adamantly refuse,
and body turned, back arched
she runs onto the next thing.

If he could practice a eulogy in this moment,
would he?
Or would it split from his lips like
the ticking, ticking.
Sputtered and cracked like a hammer
against concrete.
And he would watch it explode into a mess.
Or, at least, he could imagine with
a squinted smile.

So maybe someone pushed them,
or maybe they didn't.
I wouldn't know, I was very drunk.

19. Decision.

The lights would fall on her easily, an oiled wheel made for performance. The curtains slide open to reveal her in dark, then in light. They hold the performance, and she would accept it– the applause, flowers– people beg for tickets to a sold-out show. Vice upsells them minutes before it starts.

She searches for a sweet taste in her mouth, but salt gathers at the edge of her lips. When the sentence rings out, she watches the stars flicker, the candle. In cacophony the cameras alight her face in portrait, skin flushed in guilt then anger.

They would accept an easy casting; she looks the part. But honestly, Virtue wasn't looking at Apathy, didn't touch her. You'd have to scrape her apart to find it, beneath the flesh and muscles, because someone needs an answer. But Apathy never got one, so in years, she may come back with the same argument– the bees, the fog, the sun.

20. The Moth.

The moth went searching for some greater wildfire, leaving the butterfly scattered between the pews. The moth went searching and found the candle and the tree and soon the sun. It would circle the murmur of heat, pulled by the tremor of the flame.

The tremor of the flame can be unstable– what begins as a spark can very well overtake a tiny little moth in an instance. Or perhaps, the moth is the one who gets too close. It hears the fire talk, whispers an answer the moth has always sought.

Reaching out with small hands and smaller fingers, the moth touches the flame, and down it goes. The wings collapse, embers glowing like veins beneath fragile skin. Like paper, they crackle and whither. And in every instance, the moth will die of its own sorrow, curiosity, or maybe because it feels nothing at all.

21. Apathy.

6:36

Hesitant steps
into a swirling world of champagne
and lights and colors and laughs.
Would it end so badly?
Indulging in drink after drink,
until the organs can only stop.

Find a dusty place to hide,
oh, soft-winged psyche.
Hide in the cracks,
tuck yourself in and let
them forget about you
the first time.

Timid taps on a shoulder–
whispered pleas–
or maybe it's justification.
Chase after them on broken ankles,
rising quicksand,
and they'll point and laugh
with decorated fingers.

Find a dark abode to sleep,
oh soft- winged psyche.
Don't let the light find you,
lest it tempt you to bite.

Delicate fingers reach for rich cheeses
and crackers and jams to spread.
A knife placed on the side.
Would it end so badly?
The blood on their hands,
dripping onto the floor
from an empty cavern in their
own chest.

But a spark alights on the knife,
and they turn,
and the butterfly would try to stop them.
Wandering steps to the edge–
next to a daydreaming Virtue–
and the sun really does look like a dream,
something they tried to catch,
something they try to catch again.

Silent hands reach over the edge,
then silent feet.
Would it end so badly?
As they take a step.

As they freefall,
as a petal falls,
as a drop of honey drips,
as a shard of glass explodes
on the ground.

Reach out if you need help:
988lifeline.org

www.ingramcontent.com/pod-product-compliance
Lightning Source LLC
Chambersburg PA
CBHW051742130826
49812CB00033B/968